THE SECRET SOCIETY OF MONSTER HUNTERS

THE DRAGON AND THE IRON FACTORY

by Leah Kaminski

illustrated by Jared Sams

TORCH GRAPHIC PRESS

Published in the United States of America by Cherry Lake Publishing Group
Ann Arbor, Michigan
www.cherrylakepublishing.com

Reading Adviser: Marla Conn, MS, Ed., Literacy specialist, Read-Ability, Inc.
Book Designer: Book Buddy Media
Photo Credits: page 1: ©Trifonenko / Getty Images; page 7: ©MichaelGaida / Pixabay; page 7: ©pritharshv pushkar / systemD; page 9: ©Philafrenzy / Wikimedia; page 9: ©jooleeah_ stahkey / flickr; page 13: ©perrineweets / Getty Images; page 27: © / shutterstock.com; page 30: ©Agnes_Karikaturen / Pixabay; (background): ©supermimicry / Getty Image

Torch Graphic Press is an imprint of Cherry Lake Publishing Group.

Library of Congress Cataloging-in-Publication Data has been filed and is available at catalog.loc.gov

Cherry Lake Publishing Group would like to acknowledge the work of the Partnership for 21st Century Learning, a Network of Battelle for Kids. Please visit http://www.battelleforkids.org/networks/p21 for more information.

Printed in the United States of America
Corporate Graphics

TABLE OF CONTENTS

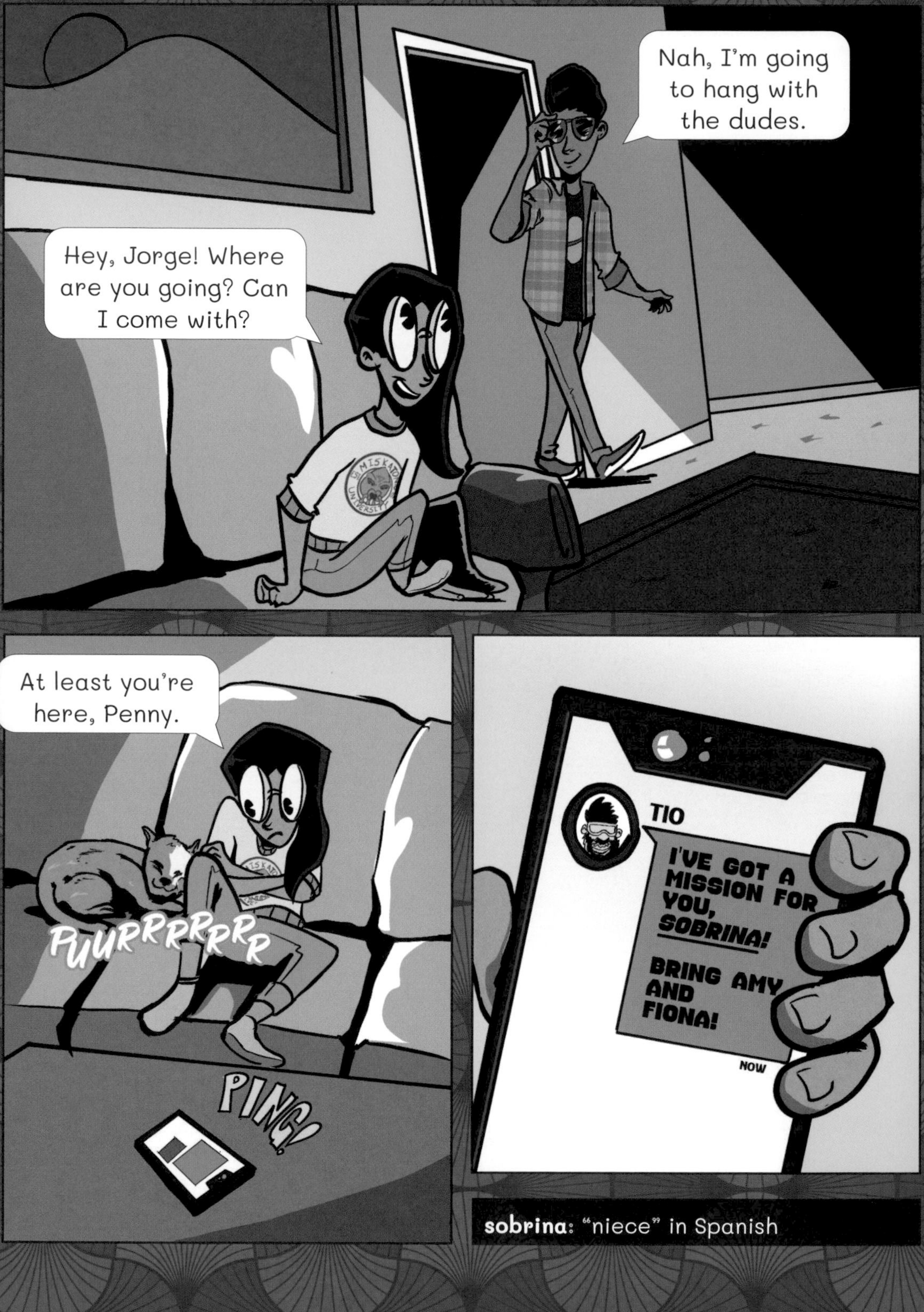
Nah, I'm going to hang with the dudes.
Hey, Jorge! Where are you going? Can I come with?
At least you're here, Penny.
PUURRRRRRR
PING!
TIO
I'VE GOT A MISSION FOR YOU, SOBRINA!
BRING AMY AND FIONA!
NOW

sobrina: "niece" in Spanish

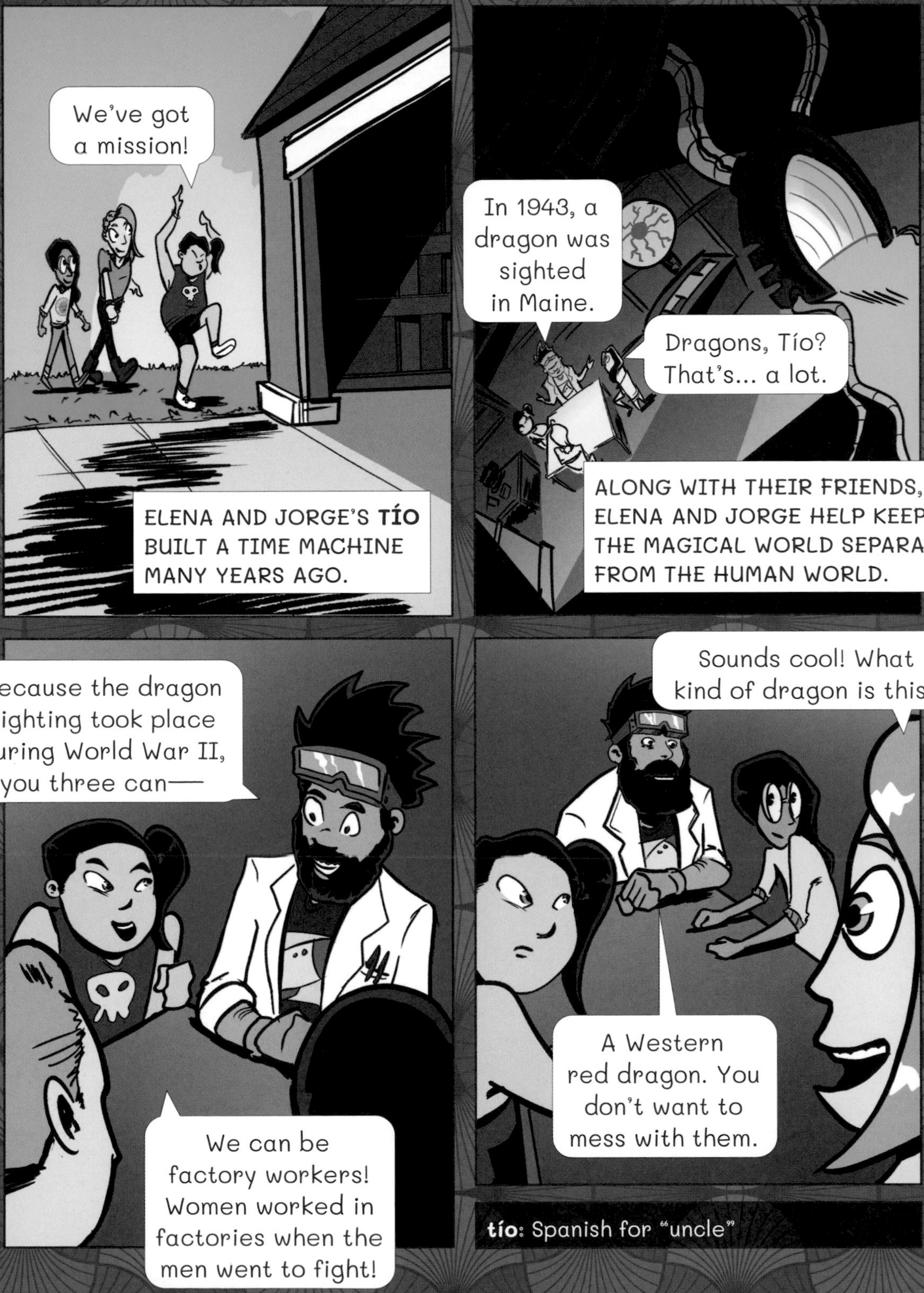
We've got a mission!
ELENA AND JORGE'S **TÍO** BUILT A TIME MACHINE MANY YEARS AGO.
In 1943, a dragon was sighted in Maine.
Dragons, Tío? That's... a lot.
ALONG WITH THEIR FRIENDS, ELENA AND JORGE HELP KEEP THE MAGICAL WORLD SEPARATE FROM THE HUMAN WORLD.
Because the dragon sighting took place during World War II, you three can—
We can be factory workers! Women worked in factories when the men went to fight!
Sounds cool! What kind of dragon is this?
A Western red dragon. You don't want to mess with them.

tío: Spanish for "uncle"

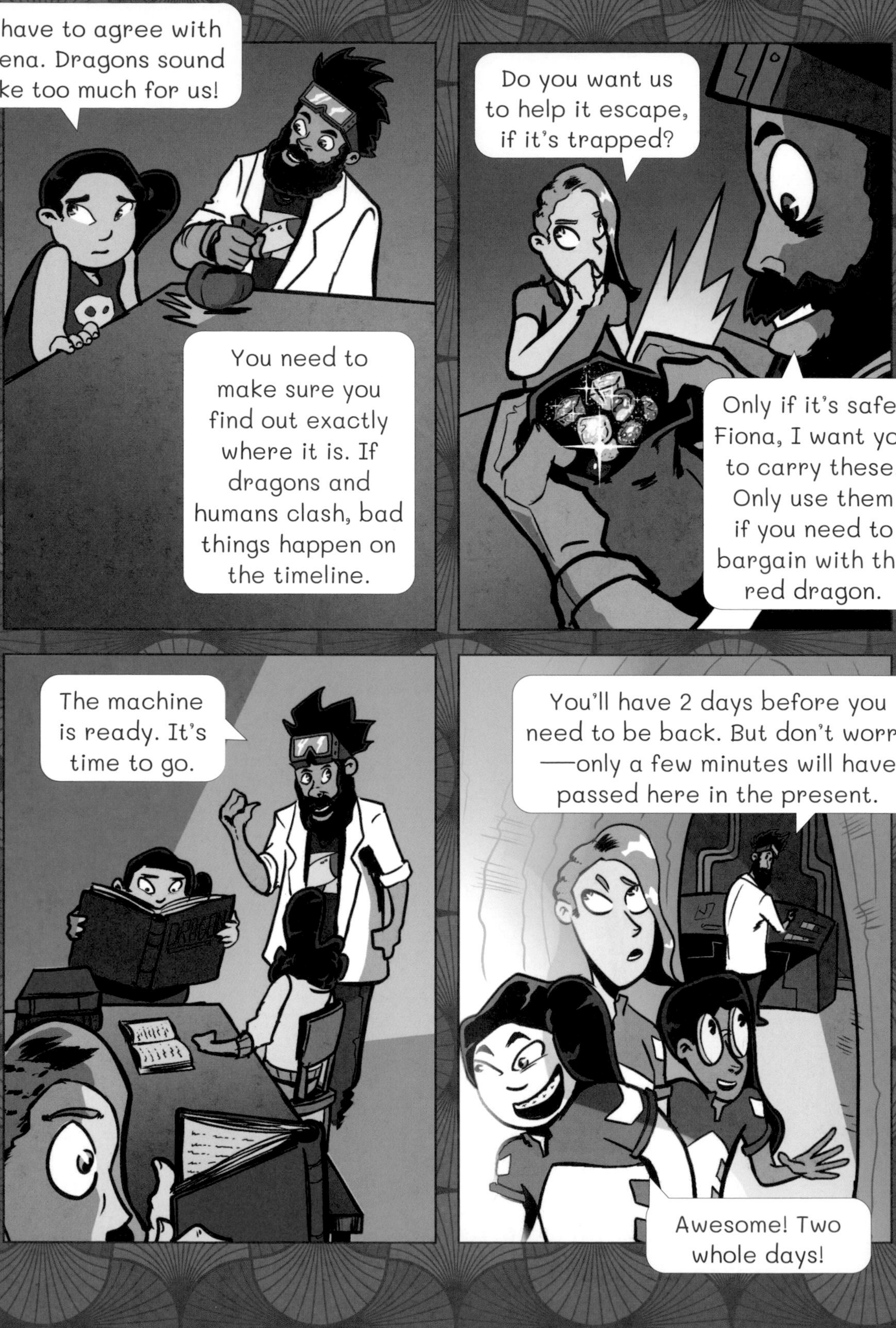
I have to agree with Elena. Dragons sound like too much for us!
You need to make sure you find out exactly where it is. If dragons and humans clash, bad things happen on the timeline.
Do you want us to help it escape, if it's trapped?
Only if it's safe. Fiona, I want you to carry these. Only use them if you need to bargain with the red dragon.
The machine is ready. It's time to go.
You'll have 2 days before you need to be back. But don't worry—only a few minutes will have passed here in the present.
Awesome! Two whole days!

TIPS FOR THE DECADE

After the Japanese attacked Pearl Harbor on December 7, 1941, the United States entered World War II (WWII), which had begun in 1939. The life of every **citizen** changed.

PLANT A VICTORY GARDEN

OUR FOOD IS FIGHTING

A GARDEN WILL MAKE YOUR RATIONS GO FURTHER

* In the spring of 1942, food, gas, and clothing were **rationed**. These items were saved for soldiers.

* Almost half of vegetables grown during the war came from Victory Gardens. These were home gardens that helped the war effort.

* Communities collected metal and rubber from scraps, cans, and anything they could find. That metal was used to build ships and weapons.

* Women worked in factories in place of the men fighting in WWII. They built ships and weapons in large factories.

* Japanese Americans were jailed in camps. People wrongly thought that they may be on the side of Japan, and not the United States.

citizen: a person who legally belongs to a particular state or nation

rationed: when a product or good is limited

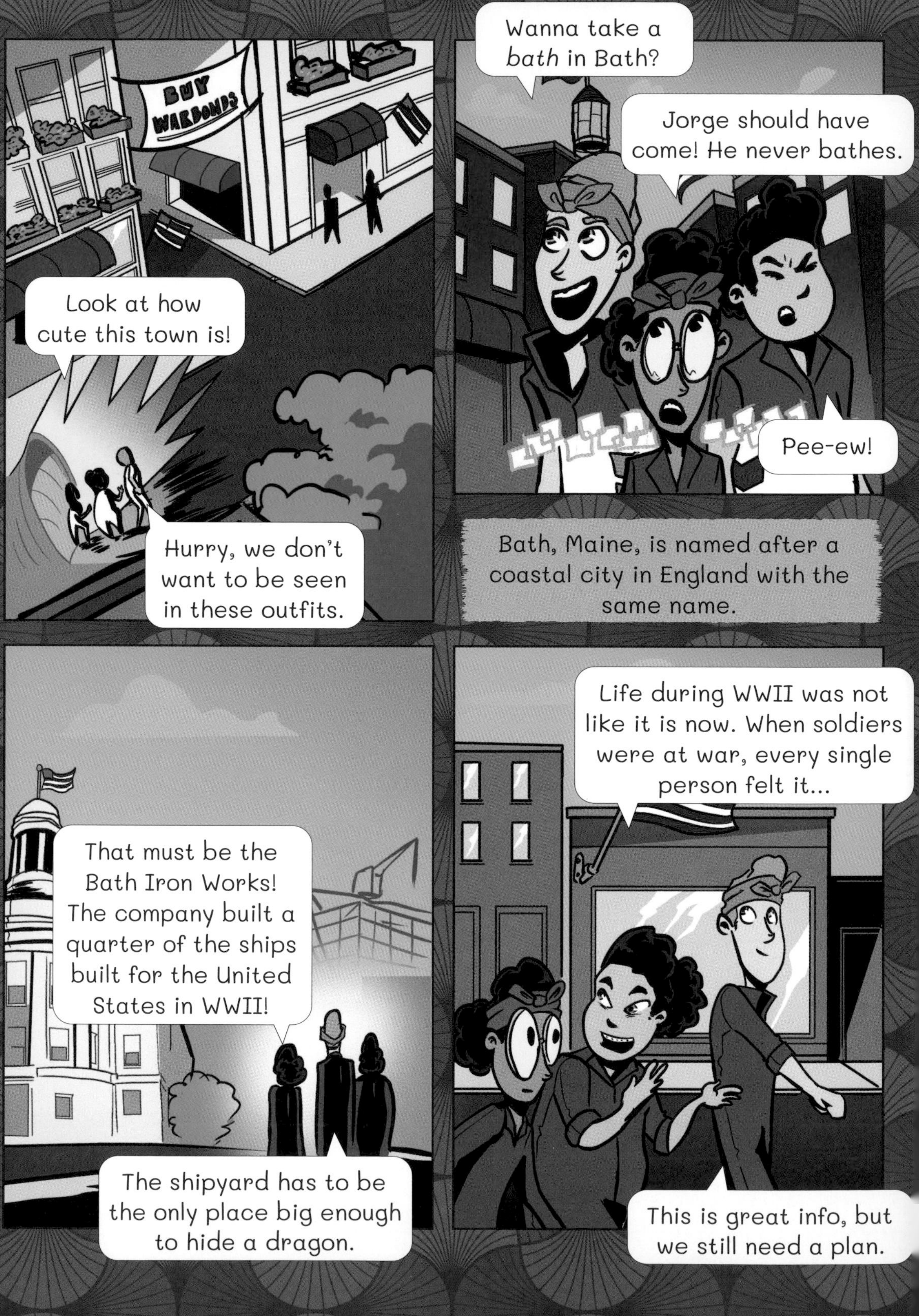
BUY WARBONDS
Look at how cute this town is!
Hurry, we don't want to be seen in these outfits.
Wanna take a *bath* in Bath?
Jorge should have come! He never bathes.
Pee-ew!
Bath, Maine, is named after a coastal city in England with the same name.
That must be the Bath Iron Works! The company built a quarter of the ships built for the United States in WWII!
The shipyard has to be the only place big enough to hide a dragon.
Life during WWII was not like it is now. When soldiers were at war, every single person felt it...
This is great info, but we still need a plan.

PACKING TIPS

Most of the culture of the 1940s was influenced by WWII.

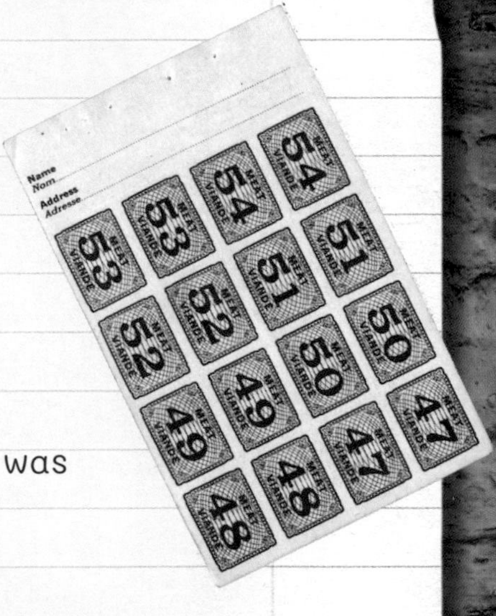

Name
Nom
Address
Adresse
MEAT VIANDE 54
MEAT VIANDE 53
MEAT VIANDE 52
MEAT VIANDE 51
MEAT VIANDE 50
MEAT VIANDE 49
MEAT VIANDE 48
MEAT VIANDE 47

* During WWII, people often had to carry their ration books. They would remove certain stamps when they shopped. Each stamp allowed them to buy a certain amount of sugar, meat, or oil. Cloth was rationed, too.
* Wearing expensive or showy clothes was seen as being rude to the military.
* Coats had a military cut.
* Factory workers helping the war effort wore jumpsuits.
* Men's suits couldn't have wide sleeves or cuffs because of cloth rationing, so a slimmer cut became popular.
* Women's dresses were knee length, short sleeved, and often had a belt.
* Women sometimes wore a bandana to cover their hair.

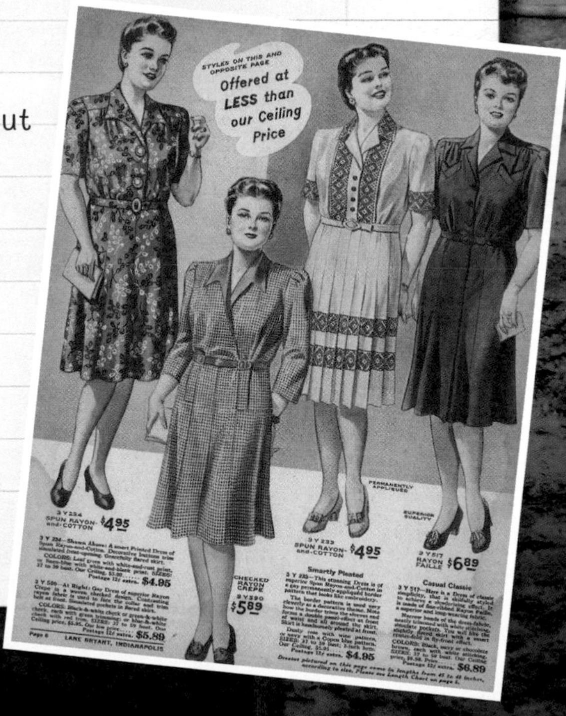

STYLES ON THIS AND OPPOSITE PAGE
Offered at LESS than our Ceiling Price
SPUN RAYON-and-COTTON $4.95
CHECKED RAYON CREPE $5.89
SPUN RAYON-and-COTTON $4.95
Smartly Pleated
RAYON FAILLE $6.89
Casual Classic
LANE BRYANT, INDIANAPOLIS

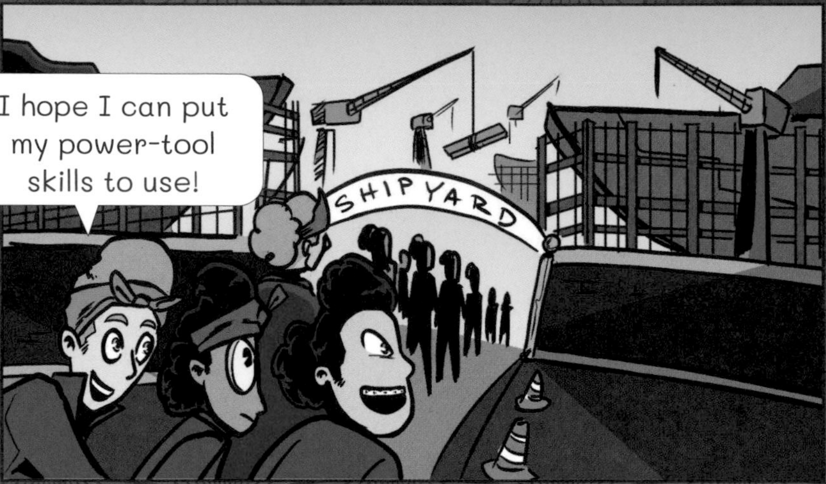
I hope I can put my power-tool skills to use!
SHIPYARD

Even at the height of the war, there were still many men at the defense factories. Sixteen percent of workers at Bath Iron Works were women.

During the war, Bath Iron Works had 12,000 employees and put out a ship every 17 days.

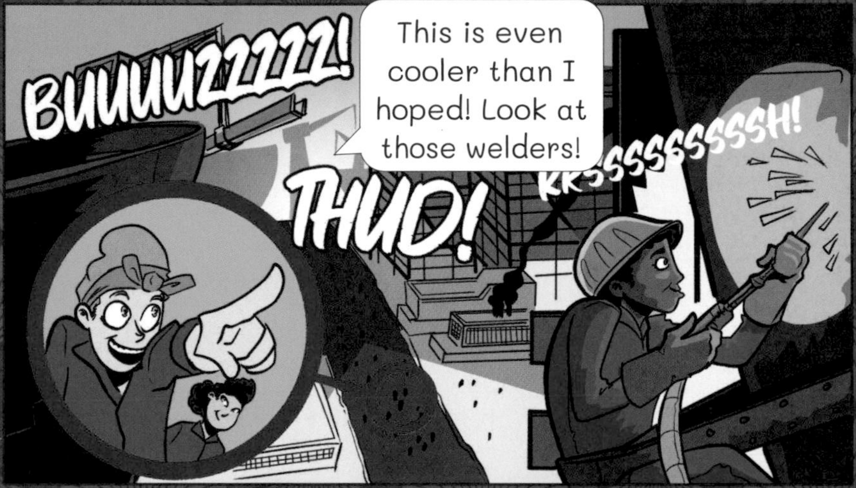
BUUUUZZZZZ!
This is even cooler than I hoped! Look at those welders!
THUD!
KRSSSSSSSSSH!

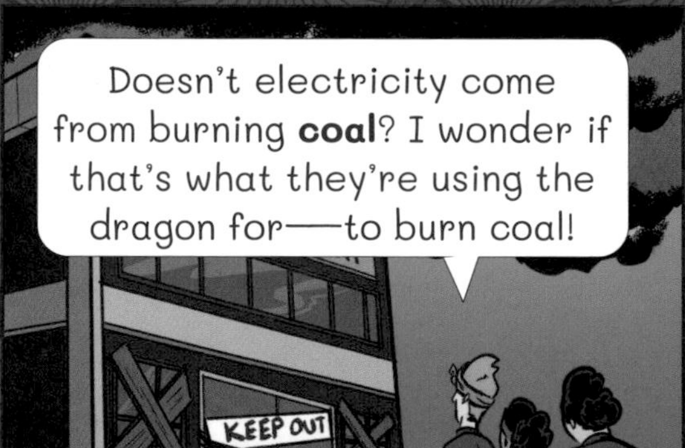
Doesn't electricity come from burning **coal**? I wonder if that's what they're using the dragon for—to burn coal!
KEEP OUT

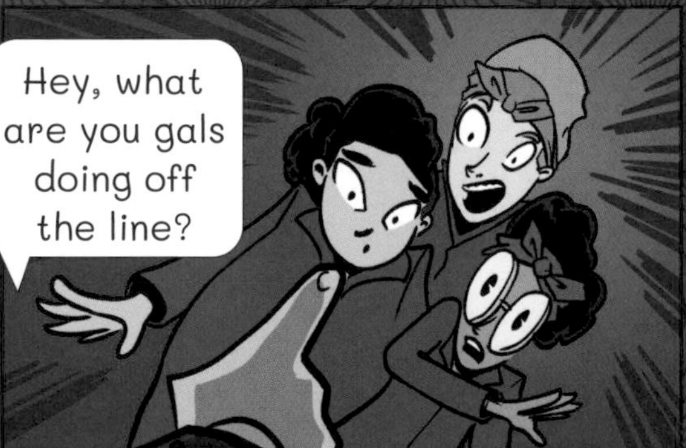
Hey, what are you gals doing off the line?

coal: a dark brown or black rock made of decayed plant matter, used as fuel

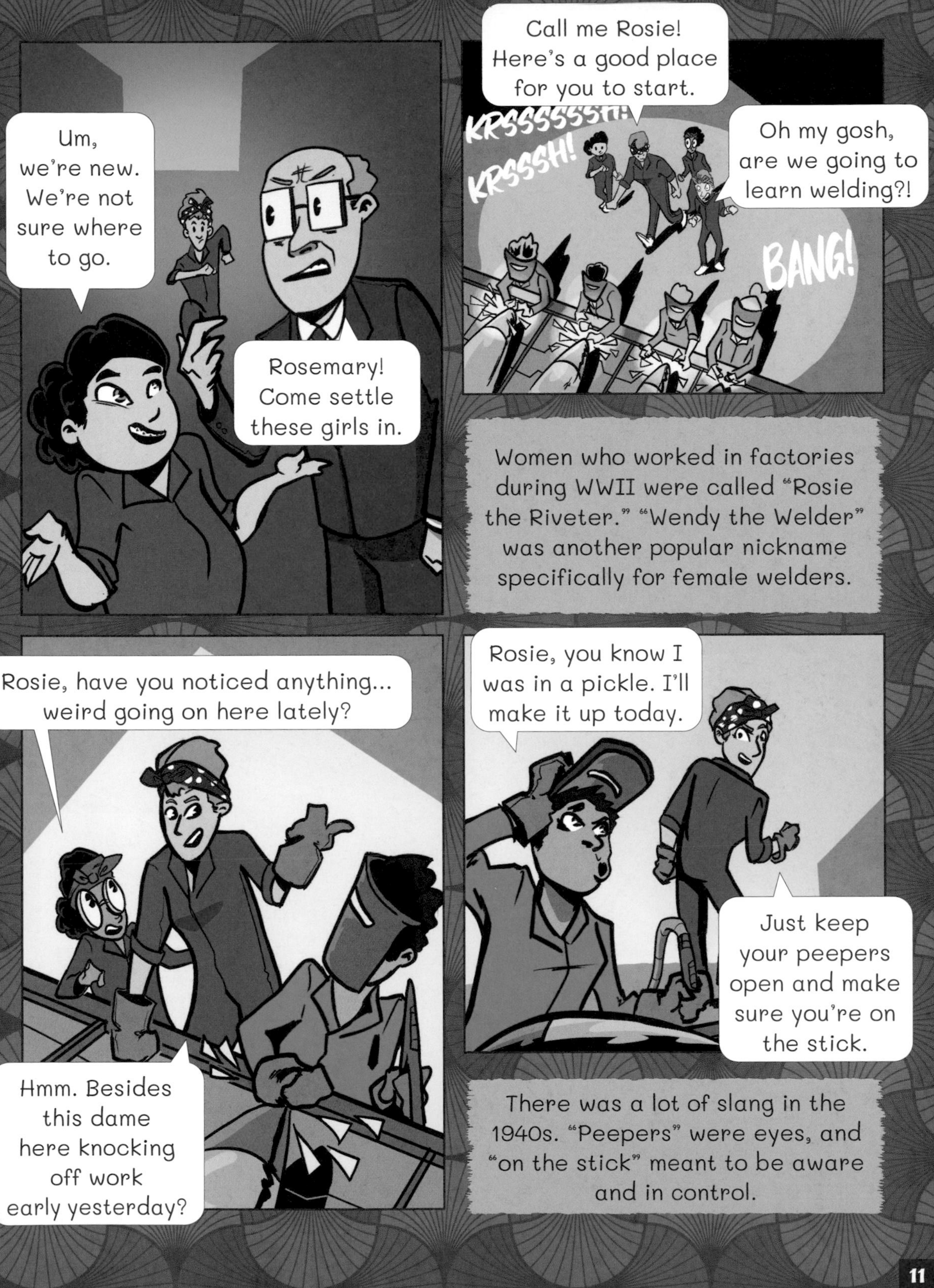
Um, we're new. We're not sure where to go.
Rosemary! Come settle these girls in.
Call me Rosie! Here's a good place for you to start.
KRSSSH!
Oh my gosh, are we going to learn welding?!
BANG!
Women who worked in factories during WWII were called "Rosie the Riveter." "Wendy the Welder" was another popular nickname specifically for female welders.
Rosie, have you noticed anything... weird going on here lately?
Hmm. Besides this dame here knocking off work early yesterday?
Rosie, you know I was in a pickle. I'll make it up today.
Just keep your peepers open and make sure you're on the stick.
There was a lot of slang in the 1940s. "Peepers" were eyes, and "on the stick" meant to be aware and in control.

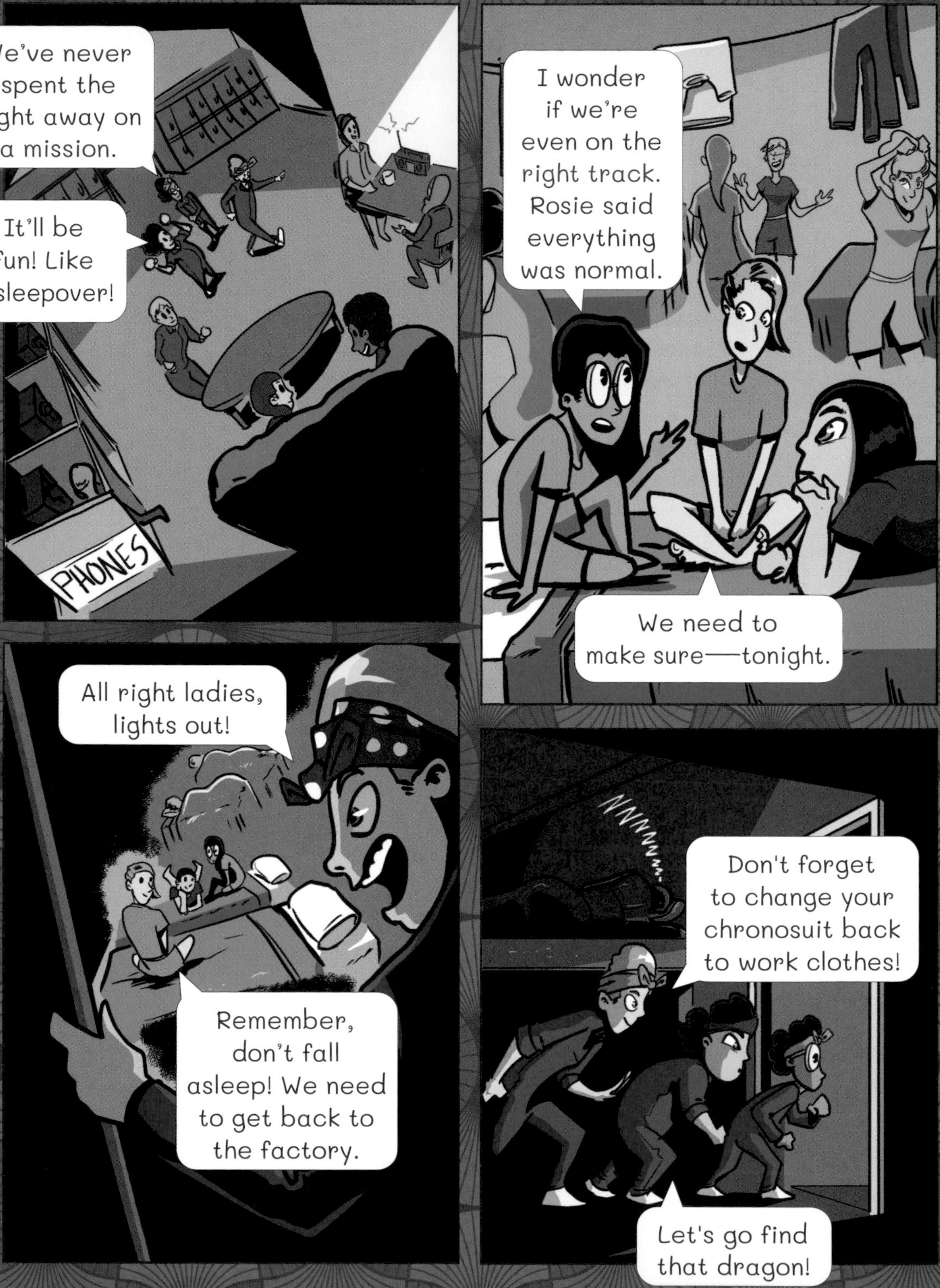

We've never spent the night away on a mission.
It'll be fun! Like a sleepover!
PHONES
I wonder if we're even on the right track. Rosie said everything was normal.
We need to make sure—tonight.
All right ladies, lights out!
Remember, don't fall asleep! We need to get back to the factory.
Don't forget to change your chronosuit back to work clothes!
Let's go find that dragon!

WHAT ARE DRAGONS?

Mythical dragons are like giant horned lizards that can produce fire. But there are differences between the types.

* Eastern dragons are snake-like, and do not have wings. They are from China and Japan. They are seen as forces of good, not evil. They are even worshiped as gods. Some believe that they control the oceans and rain.
* Western dragons come from Europe. These dragons fly with huge leathery wings. These types of dragons have horns, fangs, and thick scales.

Red dragons are a type of Western dragon.

* They often play word games and speak in riddles.
* Their homes are on islands and high in mountains.
* They live for thousands of years.

Dragons have supersenses.

* They have superhearing.
* They have supersmell. Dragons can spot treasure and prey. They can see from 6,000 feet (1.8 kilometers) away.
* They can read minds.

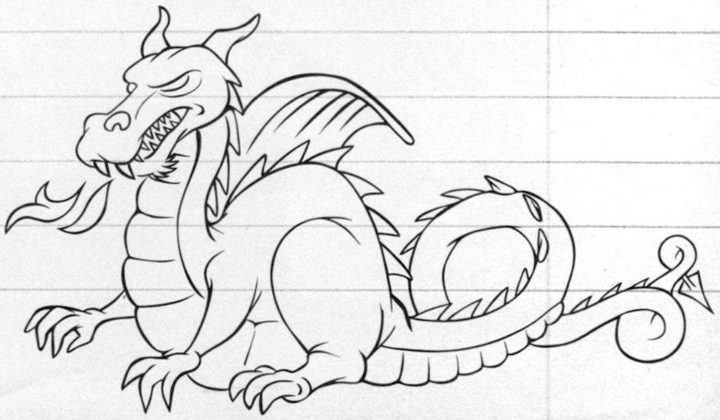

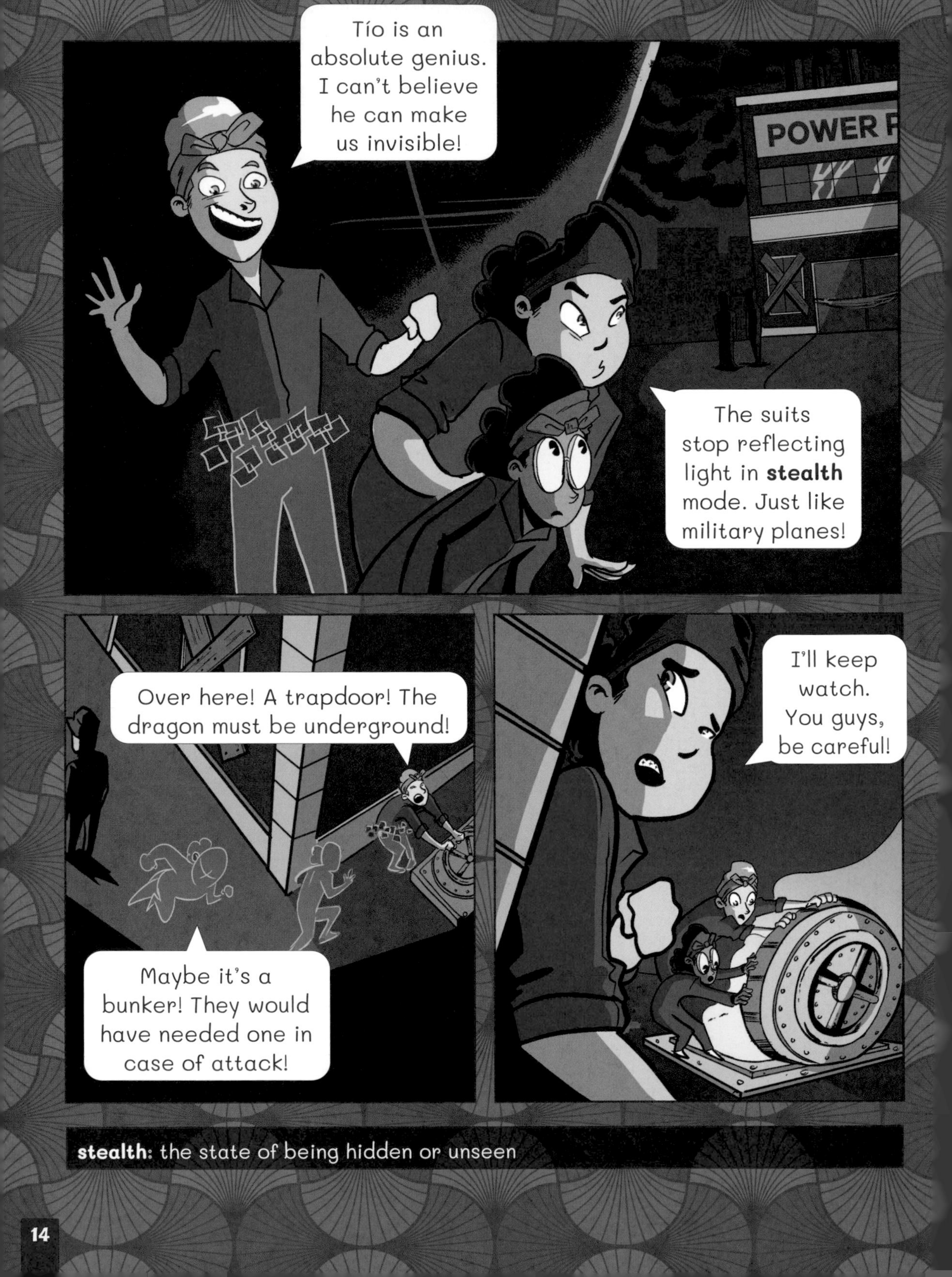
Tío is an absolute genius. I can't believe he can make us invisible!
POWER P
The suits stop reflecting light in **stealth** mode. Just like military planes!
Over here! A trapdoor! The dragon must be underground!
Maybe it's a bunker! They would have needed one in case of attack!
I'll keep watch. You guys, be careful!

stealth: the state of being hidden or unseen

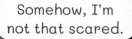

Somehow, I'm not that scared.

If Elena feels good about it, I do too.

We should have tried to find flashlights.

It sure *sounds* like a big room though. And I think our eyes will adjust.

GASP

Dragon fire can be 1,000 degrees Fahrenheit (538 degrees Celsius). This is really hot.

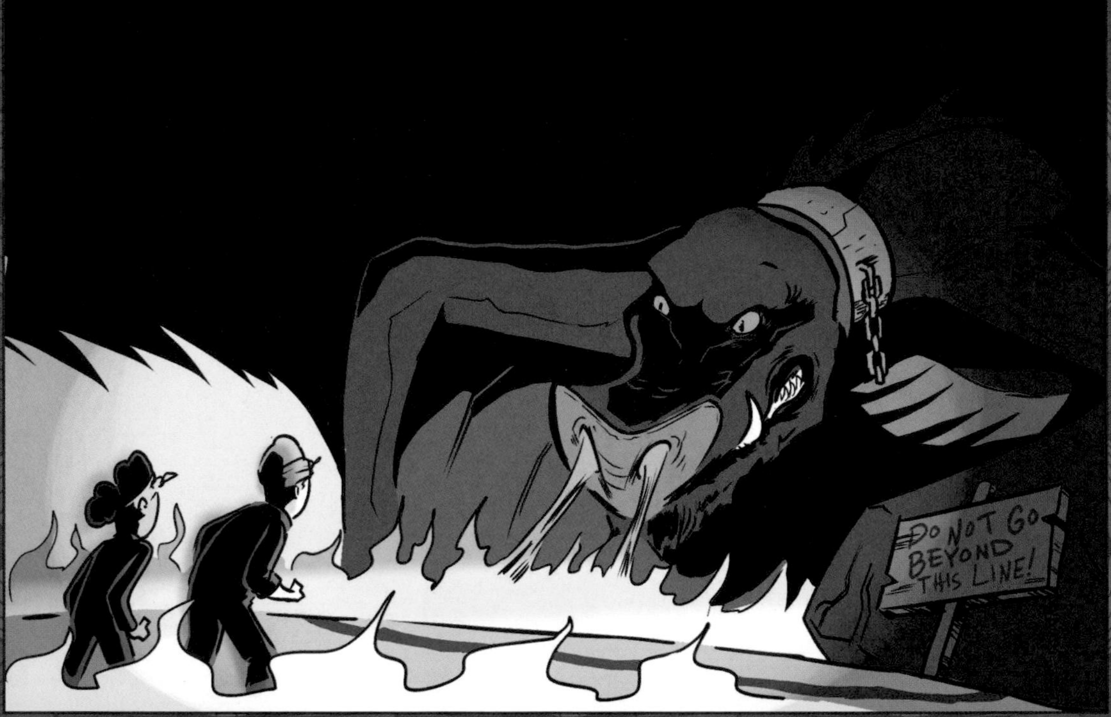
DO NOT GO BEYOND THIS LINE!

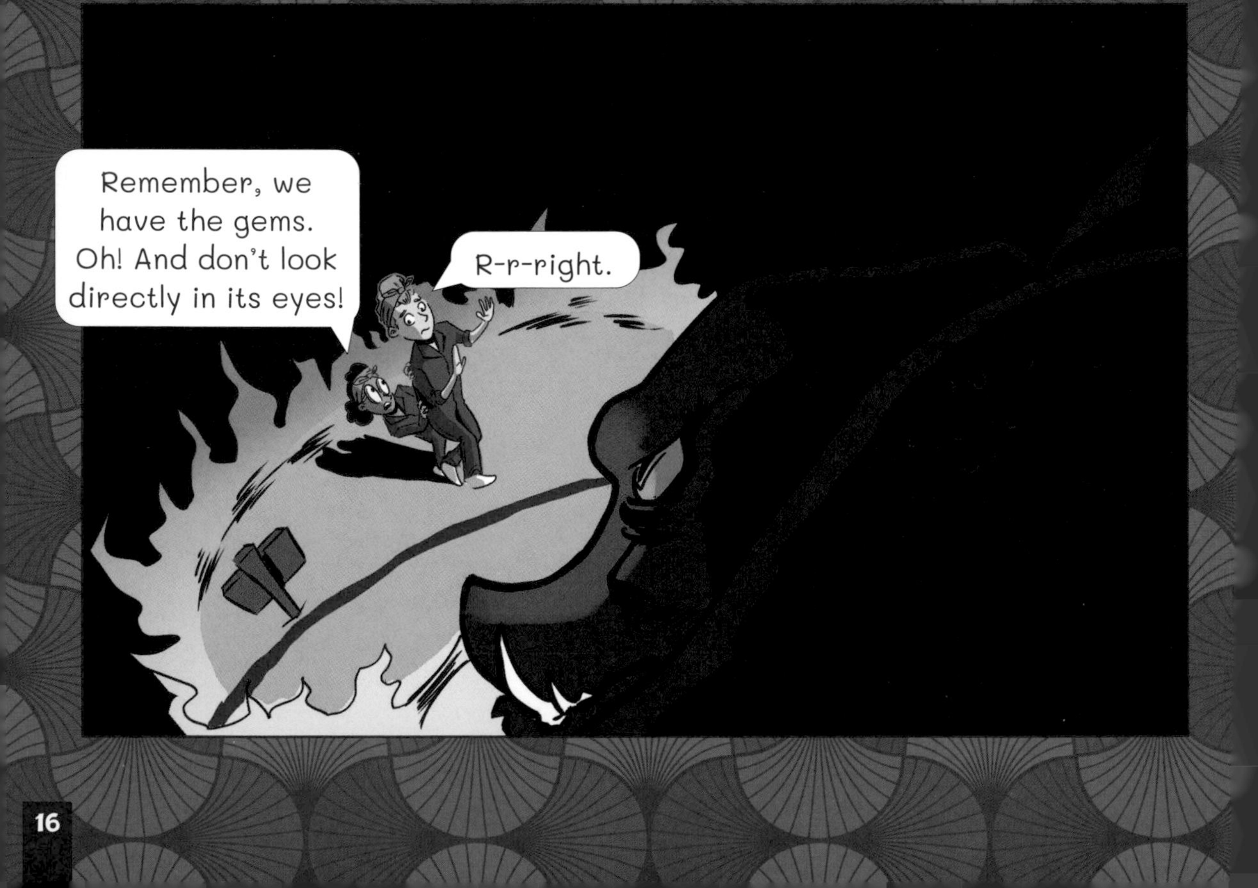
Remember, we have the gems. Oh! And don't look directly in its eyes!
R-r-right.

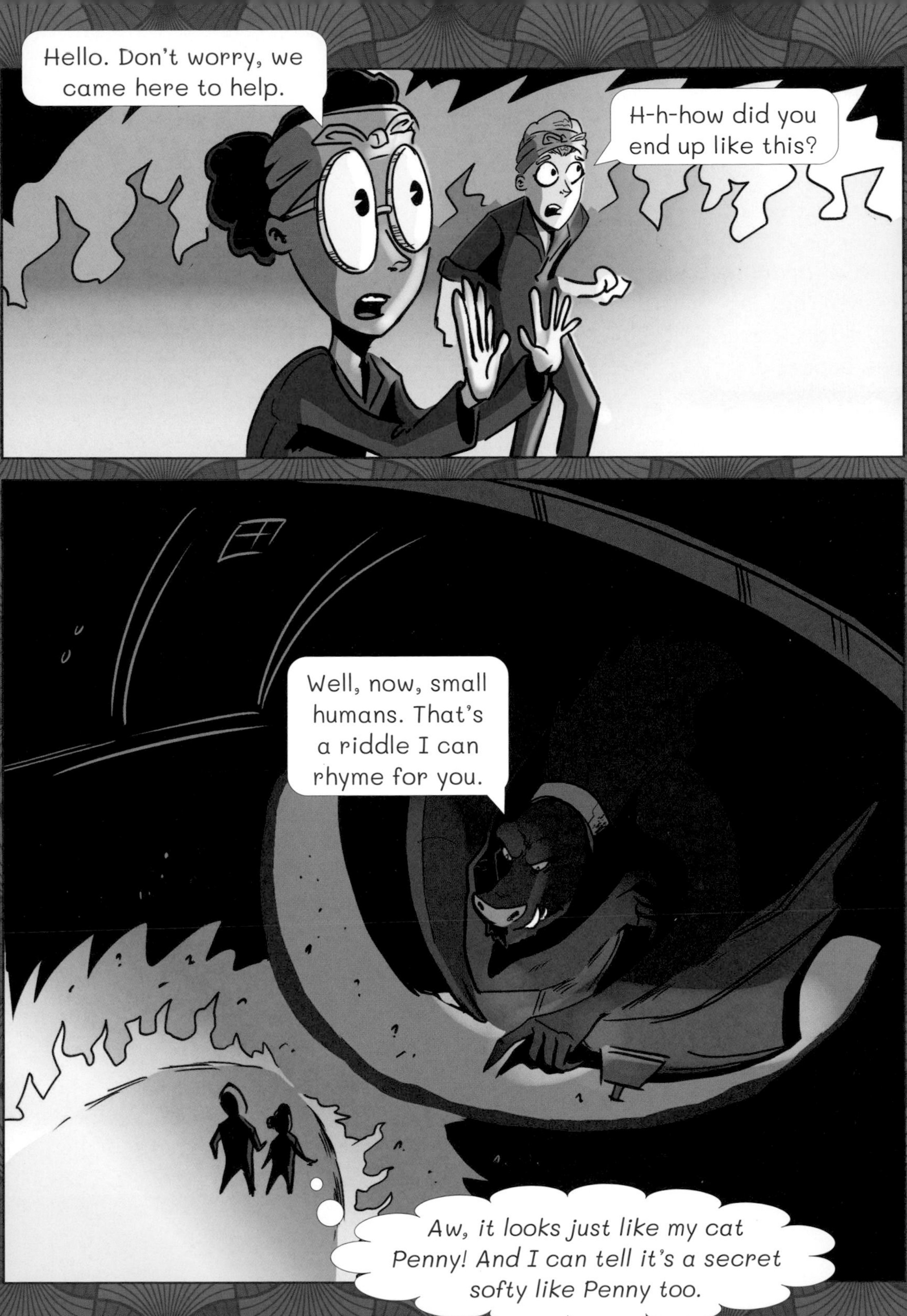
Hello. Don't worry, we came here to help.
H-h-how did you end up like this?
Well, now, small humans. That's a riddle I can rhyme for you.
Aw, it looks just like my cat Penny! And I can tell it's a secret softy like Penny too.

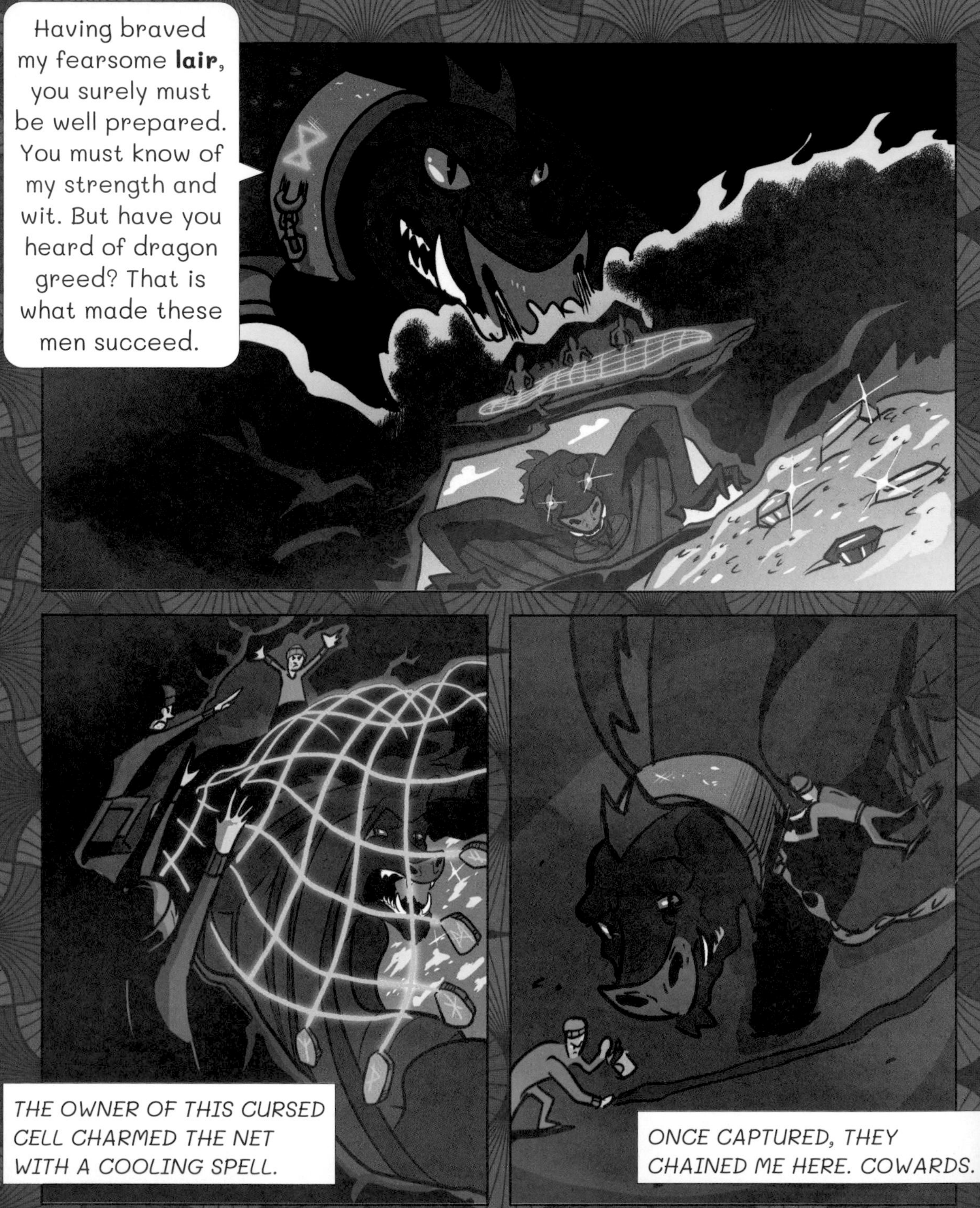
Having braved my fearsome **lair**, you surely must be well prepared. You must know of my strength and wit. But have you heard of dragon greed? That is what made these men succeed.
THE OWNER OF THIS CURSED CELL CHARMED THE NET WITH A COOLING SPELL.
ONCE CAPTURED, THEY CHAINED ME HERE. COWARDS.

lair: a hidden place, a place someone can retreat to

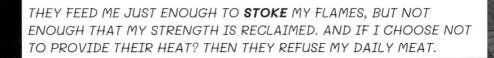

THEY FEED ME JUST ENOUGH TO **STOKE** MY FLAMES, BUT NOT ENOUGH THAT MY STRENGTH IS RECLAIMED. AND IF I CHOOSE NOT TO PROVIDE THEIR HEAT? THEN THEY REFUSE MY DAILY MEAT.

Every creature deserves to live free.

Ha! Creature. That is how a human would answer. No matter. You're free to go, now you know my tale of **woe**.

stoke: to add fuel to, or keep burning

woe: deep suffering

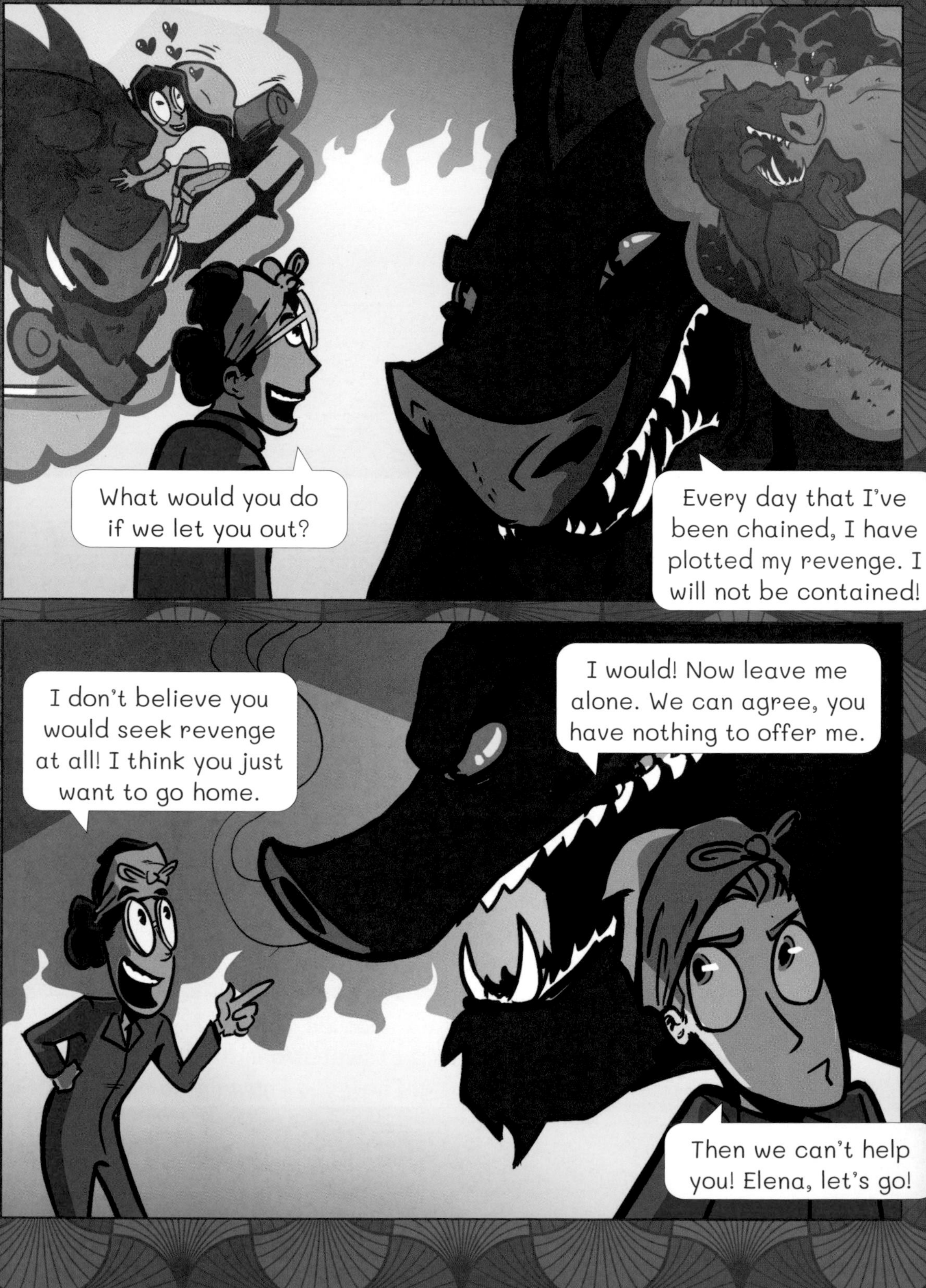
What would you do if we let you out?
Every day that I've been chained, I have plotted my revenge. I will not be contained!
I don't believe you would seek revenge at all! I think you just want to go home.
I would! Now leave me alone. We can agree, you have nothing to offer me.
Then we can't help you! Elena, let's go!

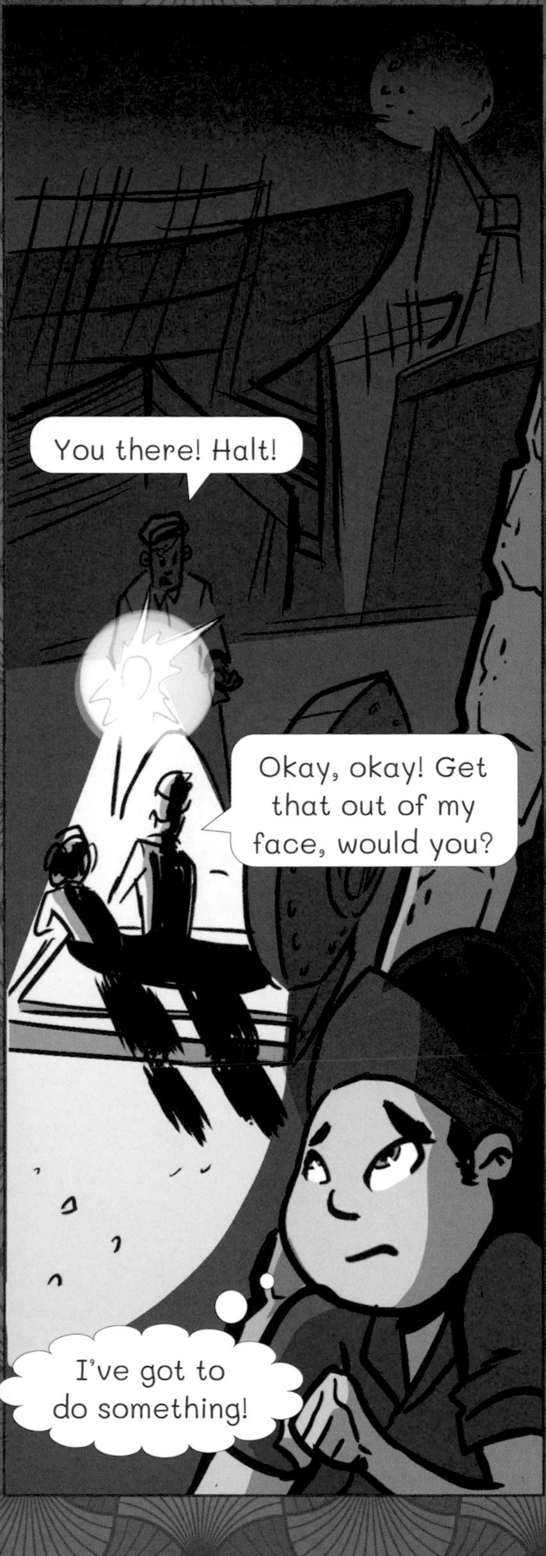
You there! Halt!
Okay, okay! Get that out of my face, would you?
I've got to do something!

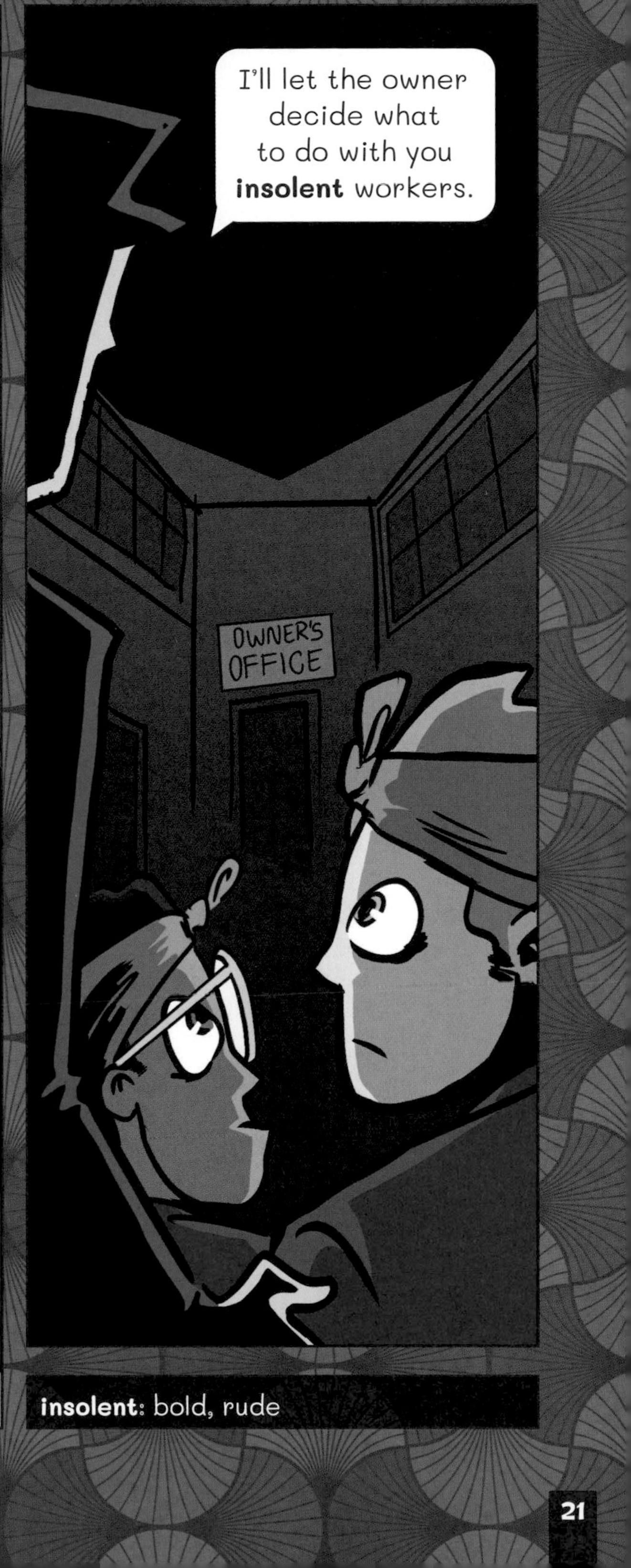
I'll let the owner decide what to do with you **insolent** workers.
OWNER'S OFFICE

insolent: bold, rude

I thought there was something fishy about you! You're spies, aren't you? You're German soldiers!

No! We're just looking for work. And if you're going to blame anyone, it should be me!

What on Earth? You girls stay right here.

WEEWOO WEEWOO WEEWOO WEEWOO WEEWOO WEEWOO WEEWOO WEEWOO WEEWOO WEEWOO

WEEWOO WEEWOO WEEWOO WEEWOO

I've come to rescue you! The alarm is a **diversion**.

WHAT???

diversion: an event that draws an enemy's attention away from the main event

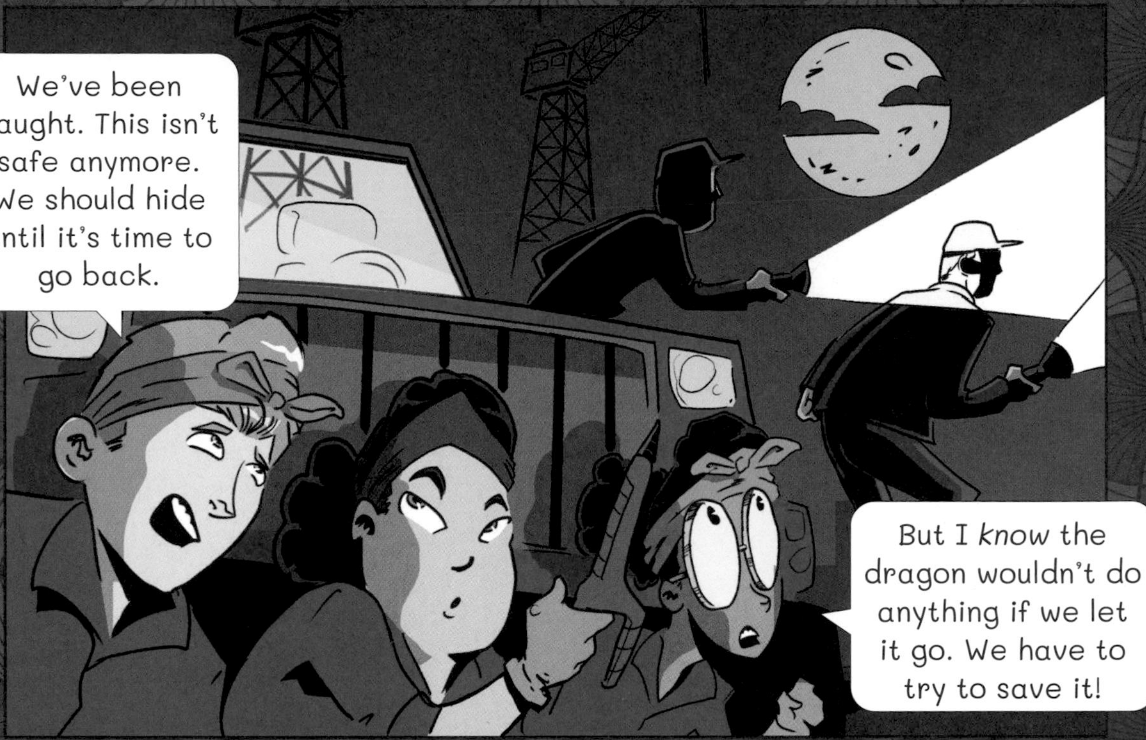
We've been caught. This isn't safe anymore. We should hide until it's time to go back.
But I *know* the dragon wouldn't do anything if we let it go. We have to try to save it!

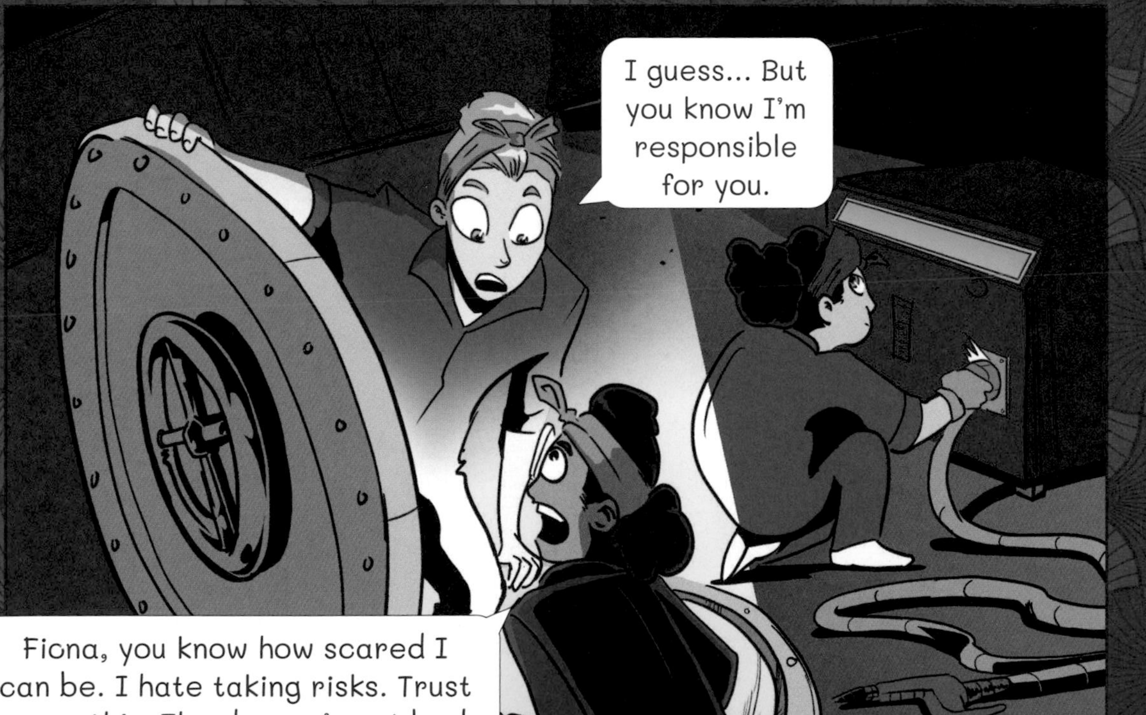
I guess... But you know I'm responsible for you.
Fiona, you know how scared I can be. I hate taking risks. Trust me on this. The dragon's not bad.

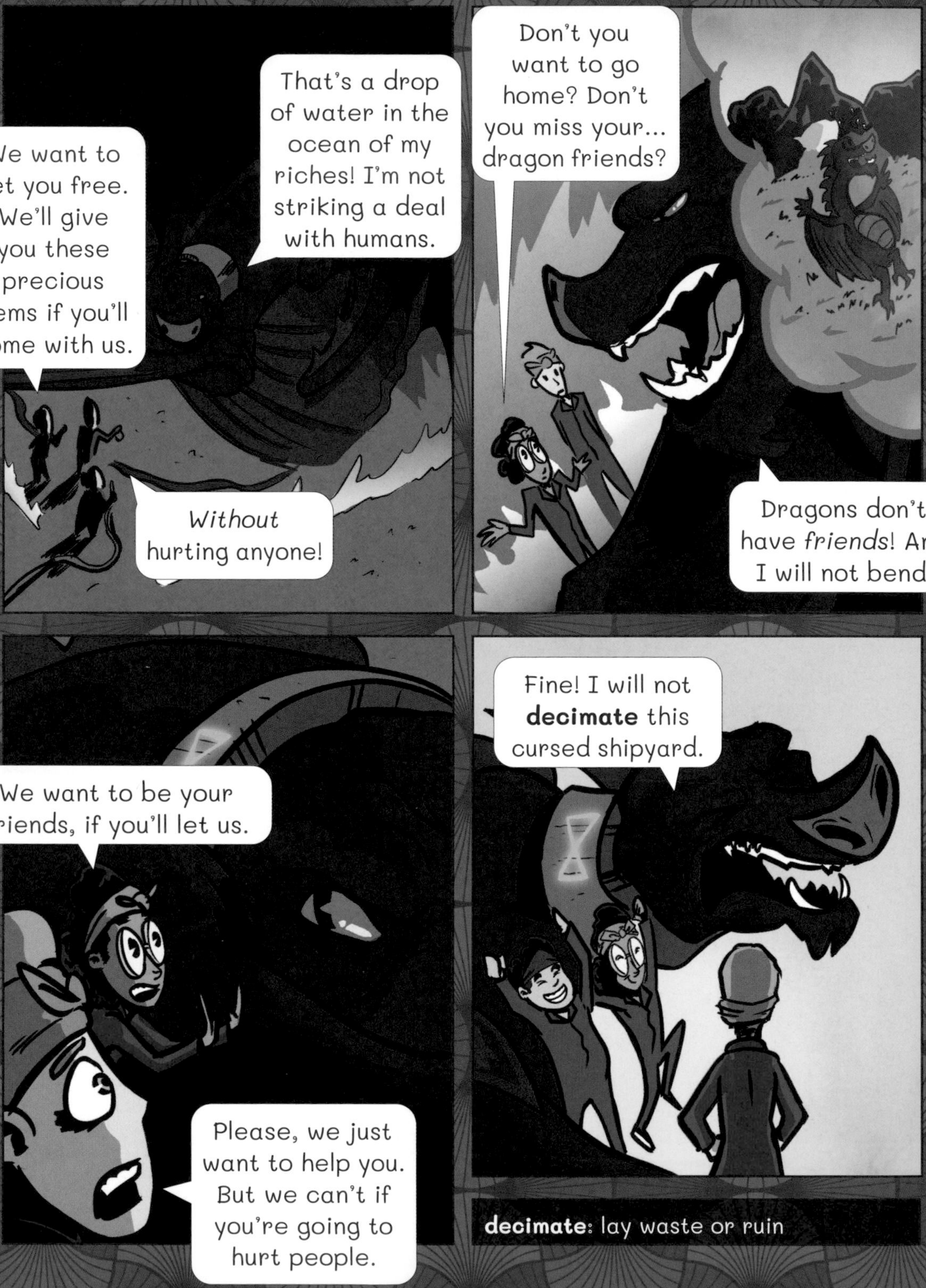
We want to set you free. We'll give you these precious gems if you'll come with us.
That's a drop of water in the ocean of my riches! I'm not striking a deal with humans.
Without hurting anyone!
Don't you want to go home? Don't you miss your... dragon friends?
Dragons don't have *friends*! And I will not bend!
We want to be your friends, if you'll let us.
Please, we just want to help you. But we can't if you're going to hurt people.
Fine! I will not **decimate** this cursed shipyard.

decimate: lay waste or ruin

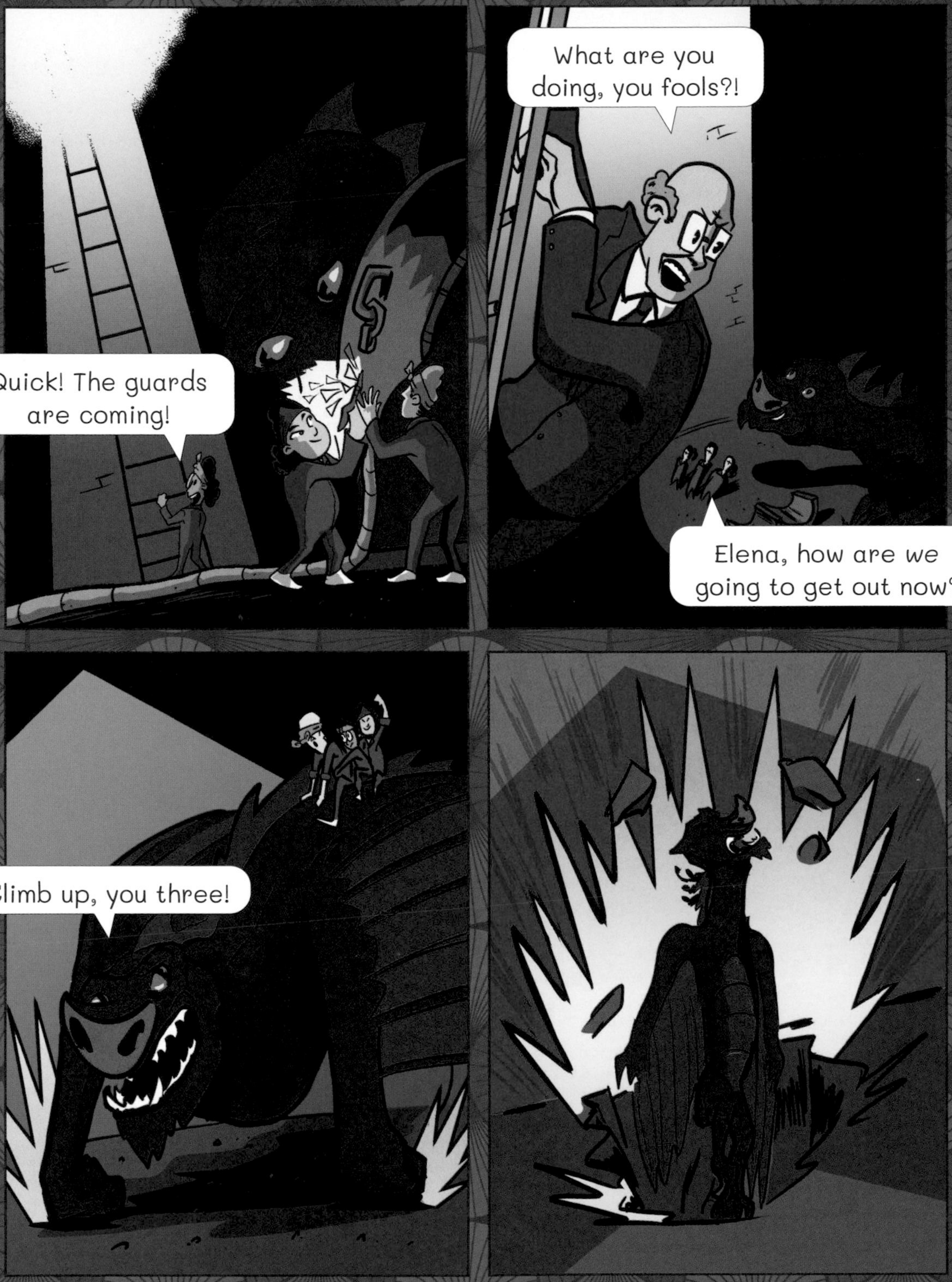
Quick! The guards are coming!
What are you doing, you fools?!
Elena, how are *we* going to get out now?
Climb up, you three!

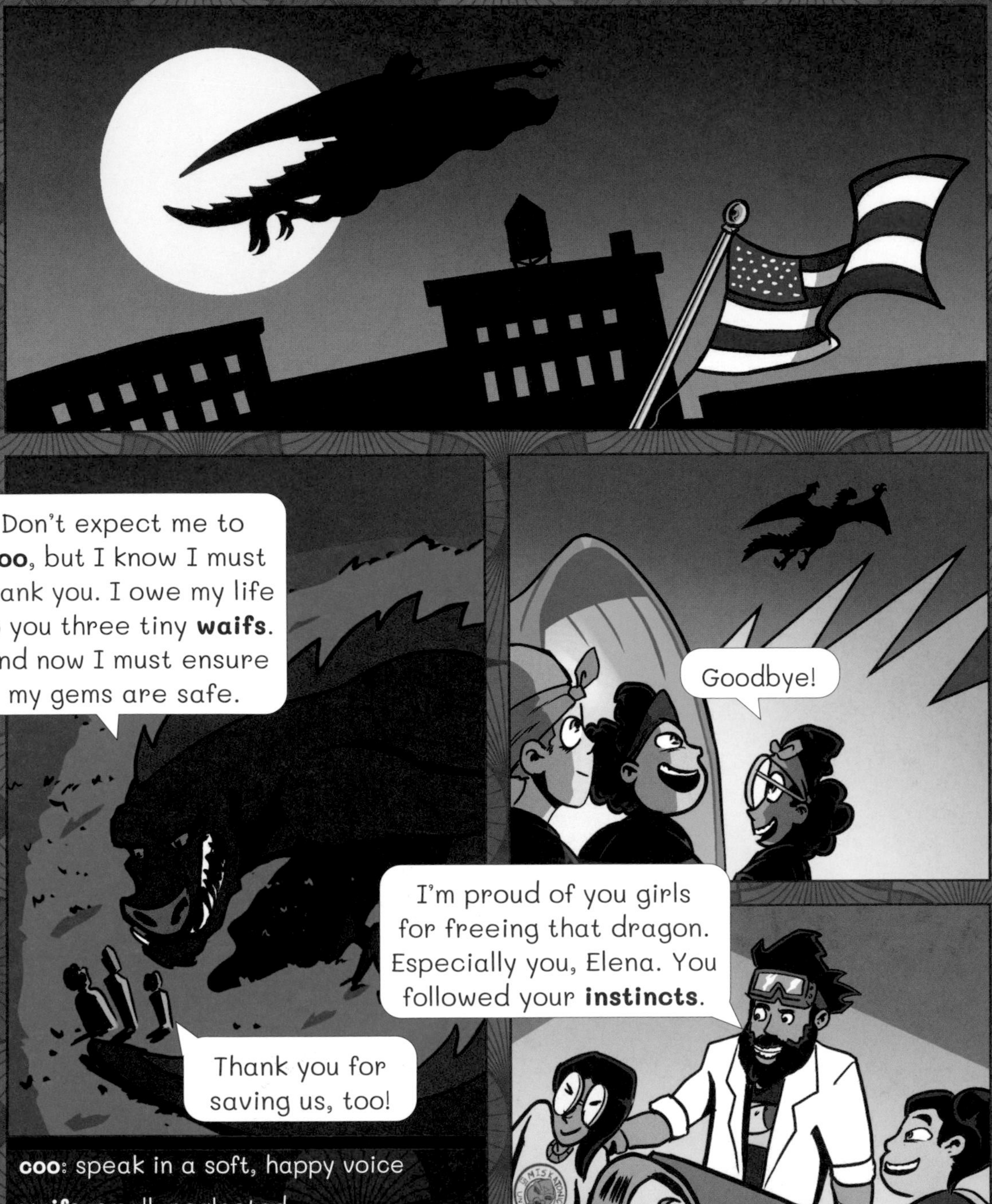
Don't expect me to **coo**, but I know I must thank you. I owe my life to you three tiny **waifs**. And now I must ensure my gems are safe.
Thank you for saving us, too!
Goodbye!
I'm proud of you girls for freeing that dragon. Especially you, Elena. You followed your **instincts**.

coo: speak in a soft, happy voice

waifs: small, neglected, unhealthy people

instincts: natural, deep-seated impulses or tendencies

SURVIVAL TIPS

Dragons are dangerous and tricky. Here are some tips to help you survive your encounter.

* Try to be friends with dragons. Offer them treasure.

* Don't get too close to dragons, even if they don't seem to be angry.

* Don't take advice from a dragon. They like to trick people. Not all dragons are evil, but you always need to be very careful.

* Don't look into a dragon's eyes. Dragons can control you if you do.

* Don't interrupt dragons while they're counting jewels. This makes them mad.

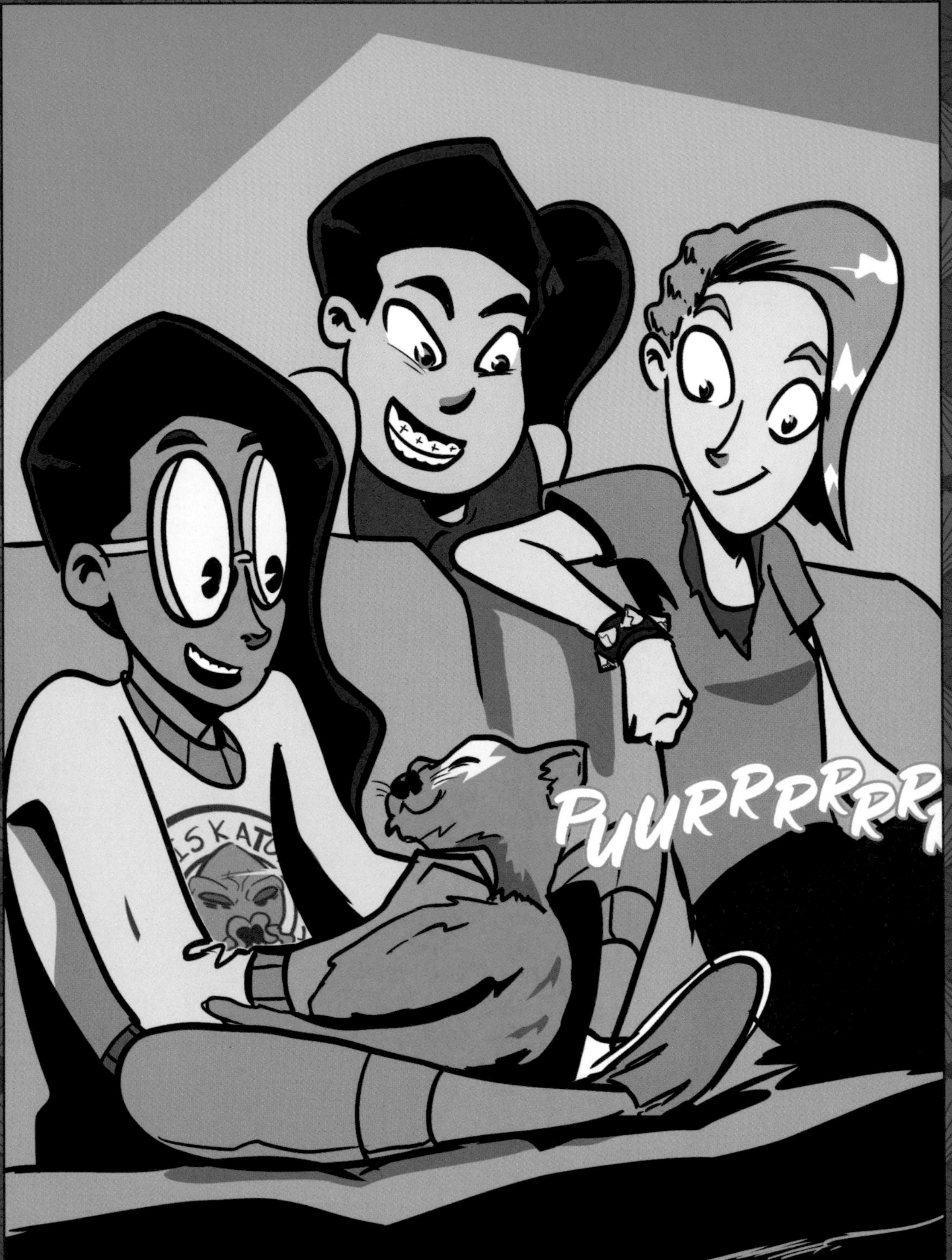
PUURRRRRR

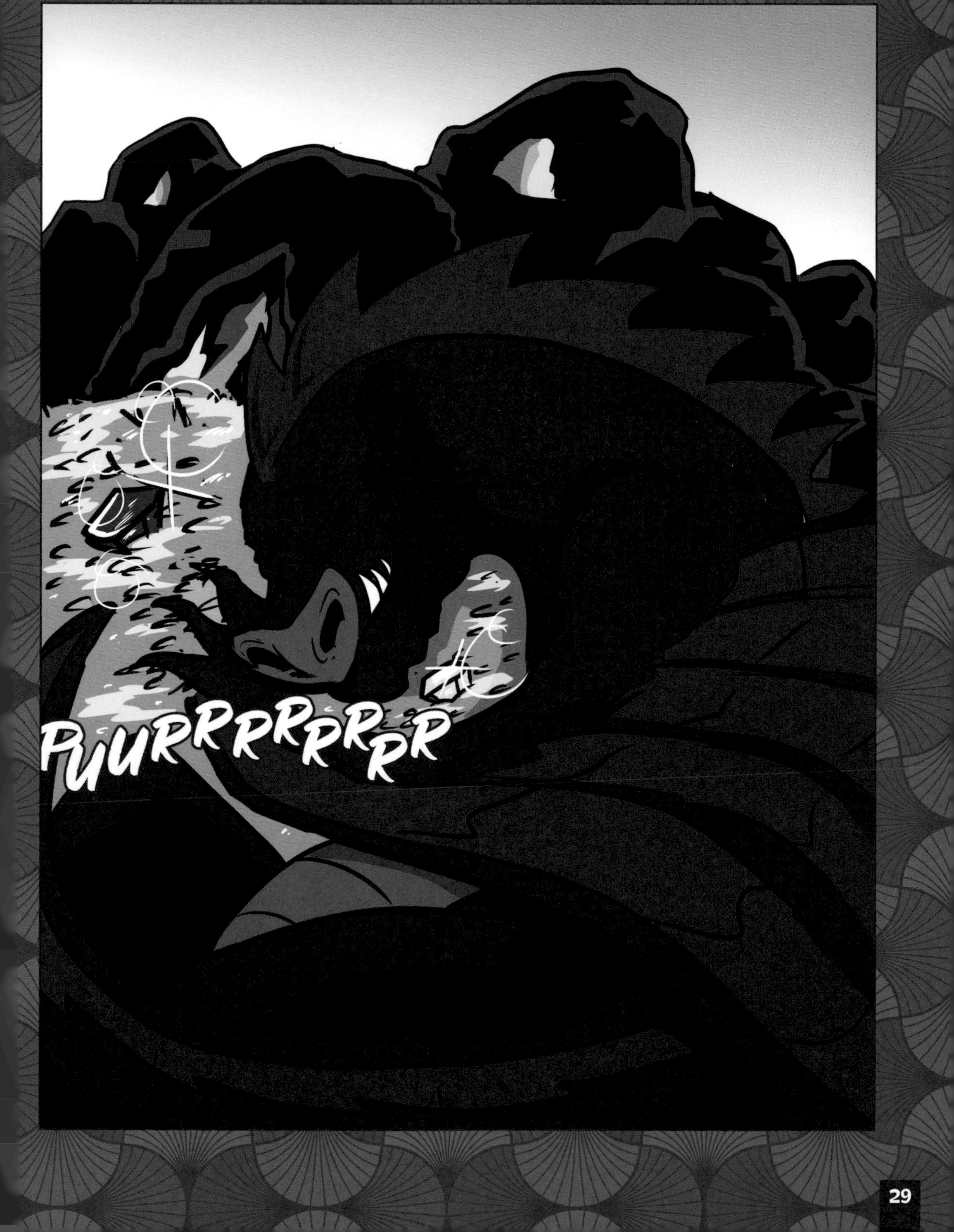
PUURRRRRRRR

CREATE YOUR OWN CREATURE

Dragons have been part of the folklore of many cultures. They have been described in many different ways. Sometimes they are terrifying, and sometimes they are symbols of good luck.

Create your own mythical creature using some elements from what you have learned about dragons.

* Think about other real or mythical creatures. Which elements and features would you like to use?
* You will need to answer questions like: How big is this creature? Does it have fur or scales? Does it live on land or in the water?
* What is the creature's habitat? This will impact how it looks. For example, if your creature lives in a warm place, it won't need fur.
* What type of powers will your creature have? Base its powers on the strengths of animals you are inspired by.
* Lastly, what will you name it? Will you combine creature names or make something entirely unique?

How does your creature compare to the dragon in this book? How are they the same and different?

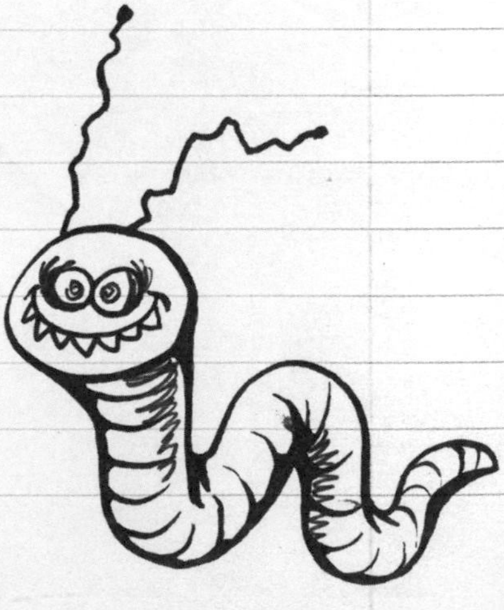

LEARN MORE

BOOKS

Isgro, Bailey Sisoy, and Nicole Lapointe. *Rosie: a Detroit Herstory.* Detroit, MI: Wayne State University Press, 2018.

Adams, Simon, and Andy Crawford. *World War II.* New York, NY: DK, 2014.

WEBSITE

DK Find Out—US History: World War II
https://www.dkfindout.com/us/history/world-war-ii

THE MONSTER HUNTER TEAM

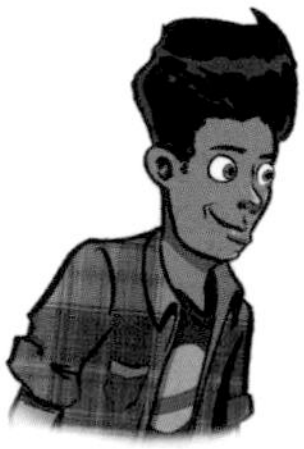

JORGE
TÍO HECTOR'S NEPHEW, JORGE, LOVES MUSIC. AT 16 HE IS ONE OF THE OLDEST MONSTER HUNTERS AND LEADER OF THE GROUP.

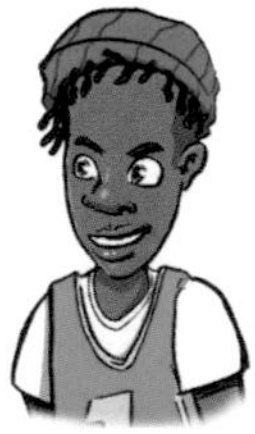

MARCUS
MARCUS IS 14 AND IS WISE BEYOND HIS YEARS. HE IS A PROBLEM SOLVER, OFTEN GETTING THE GROUP OUT OF STICKY SITUATIONS.

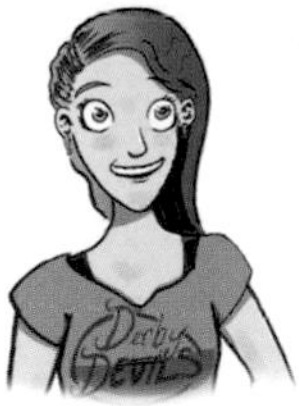

FIONA
FIONA IS FIERCE AND PROTECTIVE. AT 16 SHE IS A ROLLER DERBY CHAMPION AND IS ONE OF JORGE'S CLOSEST FRIENDS.

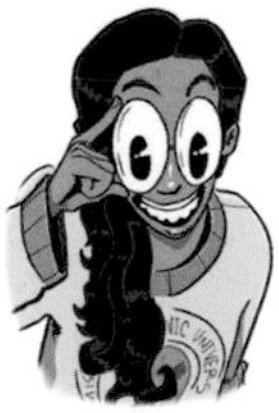

ELENA
ELENA IS JORGE'S LITTLE SISTER AND TÍO HECTOR'S NIECE. AT 14, SHE IS THE HEART AND SOUL OF THE GROUP. ELENA IS KIND, THOUGHTFUL, AND SINCERE.

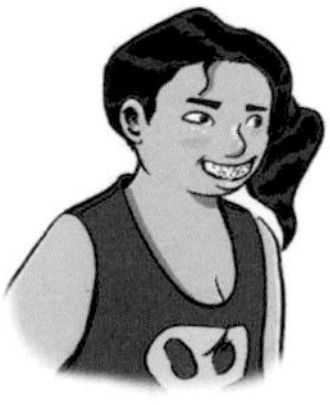

AMY
AMY IS 15. SHE LOVES BOOKS AND HISTORY. AMY AND ELENA SPEND ALMOST EVERY WEEKEND TOGETHER. THEY ARE ATTACHED AT THE HIP.

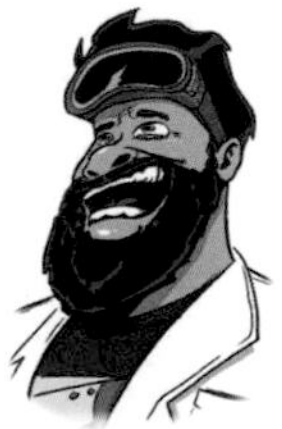

TÍO HECTOR
JORGE AND ELENA'S TÍO IS THE MASTERMIND BEHIND THE MONSTER HUNTERS. HIS TIME TRAVEL MACHINE MAKES IT ALL POSSIBLE.

GLOSSARY

citizen (SI-ti-zen) a person who legally belongs to a particular state or nation

coal (KOHL) a dark brown or black rock made of decayed plant matter, used as fuel

coo (koo) speak in a soft, happy voice

decimate (DEH-si-mayt) lay waste or ruin

diversion (di-VUR-zhin) an event that draws an enemy's attention away from the main event

insolent (IN-suh-lent) bold, rude

instincts (IN-stinkts) natural, deep-seated impulses or tendencies

lair (LEHR) a hidden place, a place someone can retreat to

rationed (RA-shund) when a product or good is limited

sobrina (soh-BREE-nuh) "niece" in Spanish

stealth (STELTH) the state of being hidden or unseen

stoke (STOHK) to add fuel to, or keep burning

tío (TEE-oh) Spanish for "uncle"

waifs (WAYFS) small, neglected, unhealthy people

woe (WOH) deep suffering

INDEX